CARVING Angels

a novel

CARVING Angels

a novel

DIANE STRINGAM TOLLEY

SWEETWATER BOOKS
AN IMPRINT OF CEDAR FORT, INC.
SPRINGVILLE, UTAH

ISBN 13: 978-1-59955-944-5

Published by Bonneville Books, an imprint of Cedar Fort, Inc., 2373 W. 700 S., Springville, UT 84663
Distributed by Cedar Fort, Inc. www.cedarfort.com

LIBRARY OF CONGRESS CATALOGING-IN-PUBLICATION DATA

Tolley, Diane Stringam (Diane Louise Stringam), 1955- author.
 Carving angels / Diane Stringam Tolley.
   pages cm
 Summary: Once Santa's chief wood carver, Papa Adam nearly gave up on life when he lost his sight, but his five-year-old granddaughter Amy's request for a carving restores his confidence and leads them to building a new sleigh for Santa.
 ISBN 978-1-59955-944-5
 [1. Wood carving--Fiction. 2. Grandfathers--Fiction. 3. Blind--Fiction. 4. People with disabilities--Fiction. 5. Elves--Fiction. 6. Santa Claus--Fiction.] I. Title.

 PZ7.T5747Car 2011
 [Fic]--dc22

       2011018362

Cover design by Danie Romrell
Cover design © 2011 by Lyle Mortimer
Edited and typeset by Heidi Doxey

Printed in the United States of America

10 9 8 7 6 5 4 3 2 1

Printed on acid-free paper

To My Husband, Grant,
Who believed;
My Family,
Who encouraged;
And my Father Creator,
Who gave me the words.

one

The old elf sat on the porch of his cozy little cabin and gazed sightlessly out at the world, feeling at once worn out and useless. He sighed and rubbed a gnarled hand along his thigh. How frail he felt. How insubstantial.

Insignificant.

He sighed again and shuffled his feet, trying to find a comfortable position on his chair. He rocked back and forth silently for a few minutes.

Finally he grunted and reached for his cane. Levering himself to his feet, he stood for a moment, securing his balance, then shuffled slowly to the end of the porch. Reaching it, he turned carefully and shuffled back.

Several times, he moved slowly across the porch.

Finally, exhausted, he dropped back into the chair and sighed again.

How long till supper? He tipped his head and listened to the sounds around him. The familiar noises that had formed a background accompaniment to his life for as long as he could remember. The claps and bangs in the heavy production sheds. The "happy," soft taps of the finer craftsmen. The wheeze and grunt of machinery. The occasional snatch of music. The giggles and chirps from the testing sheds.

There was a sudden sound of something heavy passing by overhead and then, a short time later, the unusual sound of shouts, but, other than that, all was as it had been for generations.

Suddenly, he heard the blare of a large, deep horn.

Ah. Break time. Only . . . he scrunched up his face thoughtfully . . . three and a half hours till supper.

Three and a half hours to get through. Then he could eat.

Then three more hours to get through and he could go to bed.

He sighed a third time.

"Grandpa?" The sweet little voice came from his left.

He jumped and turned his head.

"Yes?" His voice, so seldom used, came out gravelly and thin. He cleared his throat. "Who's there?" he demanded.

"I walked over to see you. All by myself!" the little voice said.

Ah. Now he could identify his visitor.

Amy. His littlest grandchild. And only granddaughter. He reached out his hand. "Come closer, dear," he said gently. Soft hair touched his hand. He spread his fingers, sliding them over the small head. "Amy," he said, smiling.

Something thumped on the floor beside his chair, and little arms crept around his chest. Then a small, warm body snuggled close. "I came all by myself!" The words emerged slightly muffled.

"All by yourself! Well, that *is* exciting!"

He could feel her smooth cheeks move against him as she smiled.

"Mama says that I can walk to your place whenever I want now," she went on, "because I'm going to be five!"

"Five is a great age," the old elf agreed. "Almost a lady!"

She giggled and snuggled closer. "I love to be with you, Grandpa," she whispered.

"And I love to be with you, my littlest angel," he said.

She giggled again, then straightened away from him. "But, Grandpa, I brought you something!" She moved away from him briefly, and he felt a sudden chill.

"What is it, angel?" he asked.

Then she was back. She grabbed his hand and guided it to something she was holding.

His searching fingers encountered . . .

"This feels like a piece of wood," he said, puzzled.

"It is!" Amy crowed excitedly. "The prettiest piece I have ever seen! I brought it for you!"

"For me?" The old elf frowned. "Whatever for?"

"I want you to make me something."

The words came out so calmly that, for a moment, he wasn't sure what she had said. Finally, "Make you something?" he asked.

"Yes, Grandpa. I want you to carve me something, like you did for all the other kids."

The old elf sat still, the lump of wood heavy and chill in his hand.

"Grandpa?" The sweet voice was growing... uncertain. She jiggled his arm. "Grandpa?"

He sighed again and lifted the piece, thrusting it back toward her. "I can't, angel," he whispered. "I just can't."

"But why, Grandpa?"

He could hear the tears behind the words.

"Why?" she repeated, the word almost a wail.

"I'm too old, angel," he said softly. "And I can't see."

"You don't need to see," the little voice came back, confident once more. "Papa says you only need hands. And heart." Her arms were around him once more, and she squeezed him tightly. "I know you can do it," she whispered. "Papa says you are the finest carver in all of the North Pole."

"Your papa says that, does he?"

"I heard him," she said. "He was talking to Mr. Poole—you know, from next door—and they were talking about the new toys Papa was designing for this season. And Papa said that he wished he had some of your talent. Or that you would carve again." She giggled. "That's when I got my idea!"

"Your papa says I have . . . talent?" For a moment, the old elf blinked his eyes quickly. Then he rubbed his free hand across them.

"Are you all right, Grandpa?"

He cleared his throat. "I'm fine, angel."

"So . . . are you going to make me something?"

He lifted the wood toward her once more. "I can't, angel," he whispered, brokenly. "I wish I could, but I just can't."

"But . . . Grandpa . . ."

"I'm sorry, darling."

"Well, you can have the wood, anyway," she sighed. "It's really pretty just like it is!"

He lowered the wood, setting it, finally, in his lap.

"I have to go, Grandpa," the little girl said. She threw her arms around him and gave him another squeeze.

"But you just got here!" he protested.

"I know, but Mama told me if I showed her I could walk over here and come straight back, that she would let me come again!"

The old elf digested that for a moment. "Well, so long as you can come back . . ." he said.

"Ex-actly!" she sang out. "Bye, Grandpa!"

"Good-bye, my angel," he said. "Come back really soon!"

"Really, really soon!" she said.

He heard her little feet clatter down the steps and along the walkway in front of his home, growing steadily fainter until they had faded completely away.

He sighed and ran his hands over the chunk of wood. It felt smooth and cool to his touch. Heavy. The kind of wood he would have chosen himself . . . if he had still been a carver.

He dropped it to the floor beside his chair and sighed. Then he leaned back and rested his head against the back of the chair and started rocking. Unbidden, pictures suddenly came to his mind. Beautiful pieces he had carved in the past. Dolls, soldiers, and animals by the dozens. Trains, airplanes, boats, trucks, and cars. Intricate and delicate machines that could be wound to produce music or to entertain.

Every day had been an endless procession of figurines and toys, lovingly and painstakingly carved. And he had loved every minute of it.

Even Santa had spoken of him often, mentioning his name at nearly every year-end review.

It had been a wonderful and enjoyable life. And he had lived it. Fully. Completely.

But now it was over.

He had continued carving, even as his eyesight had slowly failed him. Carved as lights became dimmer. As sunrises and sunsets became muted. Less spectacular.

Carved until the light finally left him. Until the darkness closed over him, encasing him in eternal night.

Forever.

He rocked, heedless of the tears that ran down wrinkled, leathery cheeks to drip from his chin and spot his worn and patched sweater. Heedless, for once, of the passing minutes.

Finally, he stopped rocking and leaned forward, both hands on his bony knees. Then he slowly reached down, groping a bit until his searching fingers once more encountered the piece of wood. He lifted it to his face and sniffed, smiling suddenly.

Ah, the smell of potential. Of possibilities.

He sat quiet for a few more minutes, content to hold the piece. To run expert fingers over it. Take note of its unique characteristics. Then he reached, once more, for his cane. Carefully, he stood up, leaning heavily against it.

For several seconds, he stood there.

Then, for the first time in a decade, he turned and walked, with purpose, into the cabin.

At first the low cupboard door resisted his efforts to open it. He sat on the smoothly polished floor in front of it, braced both of his feet against the wall on either side, and heaved. The door popped open suddenly, upending him, and he landed unceremoniously on his back. For a moment, he lay there, collecting himself.

Then he sat up and crawled back to the cupboard. Gingerly, he reached inside, fumbling around in the dust for the toolbox he knew should be in there.

Finally his questing fingers encountered smooth wood. He brushed off the ten years' accumulation of soft dust that coated the box and pulled it toward him. It slid easily. Happily.

He felt along the side, released the catches, and pushed back the lid.

His memory supplied a picture of the contents. The companions that had worked alongside him for over seventy years. Carefully he reached inside and lifted, one by one, the chisels, fishtails, sweeps, and veiners. The v-tools and fluters. The spoons and rasps. The rifflers and whittling knives. Each he arranged tenderly on the floor.

Surrounded by the friends he had unwillingly forsaken, he chose one last tool. His favorite. The whittling knife used so often and for so long that it had formed itself to his hand. Become a part of him.

Reverently, he lifted it from the box and brushed his hands over it. The memories rushed past him in a tide and, for several minutes, he was awash in them. He smiled and cradled the small tool. Clutching it tightly, he maneuvered himself to his knees. Then, more slowly, to his feet.

He walked with surer steps to the table where he had deposited Amy's piece of wood and, carrying it and the knife, sought out his comfortable chair beside the fireplace.

He laid the knife down on the footstool and simply held the wood. Rubbing his hands over it. Testing it. Feeling it.

The he reached for the knife once more, and, sitting back in his chair, began to carve.

Two

A knock at his door some time later surprised him. He lifted his head toward the sound.

Now who on earth . . . ?

Then he remembered. Supper. That meal he had been looking forward to with such anticipation only a few hours before.

He sighed happily. *Had been.*

He grabbed the blanket from the back of his chair, pulled it over himself and his lapful of shavings, and turned to face the door.

"Come in!" he said loudly.

He heard the door latch click, and someone, clumping in heavy boots, came in.

"Who is it?" he asked.

"It's me—Beany," a high-pitched voice answered. "Just brought in your supper, Papa Adam."

"Oh, thank you, Beany," Grandpa said. "Just put it there, on the table." He heard something scrape along the floor.

"What the—? Your tools are all over the place!" Beany said.

"Oh, sorry about that," Grandpa apologized. "I was taking a trip down memory lane this afternoon."

"Did you have to scatter your memories all over the floor?"

The old elf smiled. "I guess I did."

"Well, no matter," Beany said. "It's kind of nice to see you doing something."

Doing something? Grandpa smiled and snorted softly. It *was* nice.

Something slid onto the table. "As long as I'm here, do you want me to put them away?" Beany asked.

"Beg your pardon?"

"Do you want me to put the tools away?"

"Oh . . . oh, no, that's all right," the old elf said. "I'll do it later. When I've finished."

"Finished travelling down memory lane?"

"Um . . . yes, that's exactly what I meant."

"How about the fire?"

"I'm sorry?"

"Well, you seem to be clutching that blanket pretty tight. Are you cold? Do you want me to build up the fire?"

"Oh. No, I'm fine," Grandpa said. "I was sitting outside and I got just enough of a chill that I needed to wrap up for a few minutes."

"Well, I'll just poke things up a bit," Beany said.

The old elf heard the scrape of iron against iron, then the sound of something prodding the burning logs in the fireplace.

"There, that should do it!" Beany said cheerfully. His voice was suddenly closer. "Do you want me to stay till you're finished eating?"

"No, Beany, that's all right," Grandpa said. "Truth to tell, I'm not that hungry right now. I think I'll wait a while."

There was a pause. Then, "Well, that's a first!" Beany laughed. "Wait till I tell the guys that you weren't hungry! They won't believe me!"

Grandpa half-smiled. Didn't anyone here have anything better to do than talk about him?

"Well, if you're sure . . ."

"I am. And thank you, Beany," Grandpa said.

"Wel—" the door closed on the rest of the word.

Grandpa sighed and, throwing the blanket onto another chair, went back to his carving. Scraping a small bit here, another bit there. Testing and smoothing each stroke with a flick of his thumb.

He worked long into the night, only pausing long enough to wolf down the cold food on his plate sometime after the final whistle.

Needing no light to see by, he was unconcerned that his unusual actions would attract any attention. Finally, exhausted but happy, he tumbled into his bed and slept soundly.

The morning whistle startled him awake. For a few minutes, he lay there, fresh from dreams that still held pictures. Color.

Then he opened his eyes.

For a short time, black gloom threatened to settle over him, as it had every day for so many years.

Then he remembered Amy's visit.

And his carving.

He threw the blankets back and got to his feet. For the first time in far too long, he was starting a day with anticipation. Hope.

He performed his morning ablutions quickly. Just as quickly dispatched his morning meal, dropped off by yet another accommodating elf, then settled into a comfortable chair beside his kitchen table with his tools spread out neatly before him. Carefully, tenderly, he reached for his carving. For a moment, his fingers touched nothing but smooth tabletop.

Suddenly he felt doubt. Had he imagined it?

Then his fingers touched wood. He clutched at it. Smooth and cool, it seemed to leap into his hand. He ran his artist's fingers over the perfect lines that were starting to form and breathed a deep sigh of relief.

It was all true. He *had* spent the day carving.

He was useful once more.

Happily engrossed, Grandpa didn't notice the passing of time. Hours that had once hung so heavily on his hands now whizzed past with mesmerizing speed. In fact, the day no longer seemed to hold enough of them.

And the next day. And the next.

And as he carved, something miraculous seemed to happen.

Though no light pierced the blackness that enclosed him, it was almost as though he could see what he was carving. The curtains that had closed off his eyes had not been drawn back, yet the feel of the wood beneath his fingers awakened something in his mind. Something real, and alive, and . . . glowing.

A week after Amy had visited him, and chal-
lenged him—and unwittingly brought him out of
the darkness—he had her carving ready.

With great anticipation, he sent a message by the
elf who delivered his breakfast that he needed to see
her.

Then he sat in his rocking chair and waited.

Just after the mid-morning break whistle had
sounded, he heard her little footsteps running along
the front walk.

He tried to keep the smile from his face but knew
he had failed utterly when she dashed across the front
porch and threw herself into his arms.

"Grandpa! Grandpa! Is it ready?"

So much for his surprise!

"It is, my little angel," he said. "But first, I want to
tell you something."

"Okay, Grandpa," she snuggled into his lap.

"A few days ago, there was an old elf who thought
his life was over," he started out.

"Really?"

"Yes, really. At least he *thought* it was." He shook
his head slowly. "But there was someone who knew
that there was much more he could do with his life.
Someone who believed in him." He reached a gentle

hand and touched her soft hair. "Do you know who that person was?"

"Um. Me?"

"Yes. You. And do you know who that old elf was?"

"You, Grandpa?"

"Right again. But because little Amy believed in her grandpa, more even than he did, he was able to do something he hadn't done for a very, very long time."

"Carve?"

"You're very smart. Yes. He was able to carve." Grandpa reached behind him and pulled out something wrapped in a small piece of soft, red velvet.

"And this is what he made."

Amy pulled off the cloth and gasped aloud as she carefully lifted up the intricately carved angel.

"Oh, Grandpa! This is beautiful! Just the way I pictured it!"

"You knew I would carve an angel?"

"Oh, yes! The piece of wood I gave you looked like it had an angel in it!"

Grandpa frowned. "Looked like it . . . what are you talking about, dear?" he asked.

She giggled. "Papa told me that when you would get ready to carve, you would pick up a piece of wood and hold it to the light, waiting for whatever was inside to show itself to you."

Grandpa smiled. "Yes, that's exactly what I used to do." He paused. "Your papa told you this?"

"A long time ago," the little girl said. "And again . . . well . . . lots of times."

Grandpa smiled. "Well, it's true," he said. "My father was a woodcarver too, and that's what he taught me. In fact, he told me a little story about why he did it. Would you like to hear it?"

"Yes, Grandpa, I would!"

"Well, my papa told me that he always worked that way because that's how our Father Creator does it."

"Father Creator carves wood, Grandpa?"

"Not exactly wood, but something similar. His children."

"Does he use a knife, like you?"

Grandpa laughed. "No, angel, he doesn't use a knife. He uses life and experience to mold and refine us. Father Creator takes each of us and holds us to the light, trying to see what sort of good person is inside. Then he gives us experiences that bring out that person. Experiences that carve off the rough, unwanted edges and slowly shape and refine us until we are perfect."

"Oh." A short silence. "I don't get it," she whispered.

Grandpa laughed. "That's all right, angel. You will." He lifted her to her feet. "Now, I've saved something special from my breakfast, just for our mid-morning snack. Want to share it with me?"

"Oh, yes, Grandpa!" The little girl grabbed the old elf's hand and towed him into the cabin.

Three

Soon it became common for Amy to come by, bringing him choice pieces of wood she had found. The two of them would chat while he carved, share something from his breakfast or lunch, and then Amy would disappear as quickly as she had come.

Soon a little parade of figures—animals, people, machines, toys, and games, lined the shelves of the old elf's home. Each one beautifully and lovingly carved.

Each one perfect.

And with each, the old elf's joy increased.

One day Amy appeared as usual and handed her grandfather yet another piece of wood.

He took it with gentle fingers. "And what do you see in this piece, angel?" he asked.

"A horse," she answered promptly.

"Really? A horse?"

"Yes, but raised up on his hind legs and sort of . . . waving his front feet in the air. And his hair all flying out."

"Hmmm," her grandpa said thoughtfully. He ran his fingers over the piece of wood. "I see what you mean," he said slowly. "But I don't think he wants to come out of the wood for me."

"What? Of course he does, Grandpa. They all do!"

"No. I think this little fellow wants to come out for you, angel," he said.

She was silent for a moment. "For me?"

"Yes, for you." Grandpa smiled. "And I'd like to teach you, if you'd like to learn."

"But it takes sharp knives, Grandpa," she said doubtfully. "I'm not supposed to use sharp knives."

Grandpa laughed. "Well, not normally, but I will teach you how to use them properly. I think five years old is the right time to learn."

She giggled. "All right, Grandpa. Teach me!"

He handed the wood to her and told her to touch it.

She took it in her little hands and turned it over and over. "It's so pretty, Grandpa," she said. "I can see the horse. He's right there. There's his feet. And his head. Oh, Grandpa, he has such a long, beautiful tail!"

Grandpa smiled. "Now I want to show you my favorite knife," he said. He took a small tool and pressed it into her hand. "Now this is how you hold it," he said, moving the little fingers. "If you always take it like this, you won't ever hurt yourself." He held out his hand. "Now hand me your wood."

The little girl slid her wood over to the searching fingers.

"Now, hold it like this," he said, moving the piece. "And make sure you take it firmly. Always like this," he demonstrated, " . . . and you will never have any trouble."

"Now I can carve?" she asked.

"Yes. Now you can carve."

And she did.

From then on, whenever she came to visit, both of them would sit together and carve while they talked.

Gradually, her horse emerged. Not quite as her grandpa would have carved it, but still very beautiful. And after that came many other animals and birds, each a little more perfect than the last.

There were the occasional mishaps. Once, Amy slipped and poked a hole in her thumb. And once, even more disastrously, she poked a hole in the figure she was carving.

"Grandpa?' she asked later.

"What is it, angel?"

"Why is it so much easier for the hole in my thumb to heal than it is for the hole in my bird?"

Grandpa smiled. "Well, that's just how Father Creator made us," he said.

"So we would heal?"

"Exactly. So we would heal. He knew that we would have mishaps in our lives. And he provided for that."

"He thinks of everything," Amy said.

"He certainly does." Grandpa smiled.

They carved in silence for a few minutes.

"Grandpa, this part is hard." The little girl held her carving out and put her grandfather's hand on it.

"What's the matter, dear?"

"The bird's beak," she said. "It's so tiny."

"Ah. Yes, well, you'll find that the smaller the piece, the more difficult."

"Huh?"

"When things are more delicate . . . tiny . . . it's harder to work."

The little girl sighed. "I know."

"But the tiny work is what takes a piece from nice to beautiful."

"Grandpa, you always say funny things!"

"Let me help you with the beak," he said, smiling patiently.

For a few minutes, they were silent once more. The only sound, the scrape of Grandpa's knife.

Finally he handed it back. "What do you think of that?"

"Oh, Grandpa, it's perfect!" she crowed. Then she sighed. "Will I ever get as good as you?"

"Oh, darling, you'll be much, much better than me!"

"I don't want to be better. Just perfect. Like you."

He smiled. "I'm far from perfect, dear."

"Well, *I* think you're perfect!"

Grandpa was silent for a moment. Then he said, "And that's something else that Father Creator did for me," he said softly. "He has proved to me that he thinks I am still important."

"Did he do that?"

"Oh, yes, angel. Through you."

"Oh."

They carved on in silence for several minutes. The tick of the old clock in the corner and the scrape of knives were loud in the stillness.

Then another sound intruded. The whistle of wind as something large passed by overhead.

Grandpa looked up. "Sounds like they're getting the sleigh ready," he said.

Amy stopped carving. "Yeah, they are," she said. "But they're all worried about it."

"Worried? Why?"

"Well . . . I think there's something wrong with it," she said. "Papa was talking to some other elves on our front porch the other night, and they said they don't know if the sleigh will make it through another year."

"Not make it?" Grandpa's face creased into a frown. "What's wrong with it?"

"It's old," Amy said simply.

"Ah." Grandpa half-smiled. "Another relic," he said softly.

"What?"

"Nothing, darling, just Grandpa talking to himself."

"Oh."

Sometime later, the little girl set her carving down and began to scrape up her shavings.

Her grandfather turned toward her. "Getting ready to go, angel?" he asked.

"Yeah. The day-end whistle went," she told him.

"Huh. I didn't even hear it," Grandpa said wonderingly.

"And I promised Mama I'd be home for supper."

"Better scoot!"

She giggled. "Grandpa, you say the funniest things!" She threw her arms around him. "Mmmm, you smell nice," she said, "like fresh wood and peppermint."

He laughed. "That's what grandpas are made of," he said, hugging her back. "Will I see you tomorrow?"

"Oh, yes, Grandpa! I want to finish this bird for Mama for Christmas!"

"But Christmas is still months away!"

"That's okay!"

"Well, all right then."

Another hug. "I love you, Grandpa!"

"I love you, too, dear . . . so much!"

And she was gone.

Grandpa carefully tidied up the room and threw a cloth over the tools set in regimental order on the table. Then he moved his chair over to the fire and sat down. For several minutes, he rocked, listening to the ticking of the clock and the sounds of evening coming in through the open kitchen window.

Some final tweets and wheezes from the testing shed. The click of tools being shelved or hung. Someone sweeping.

Some good-natured bantering from workers heading home.

"So, Beany, is that dinner for Papa Adam?"

"It is," came Beany's cheerful voice.

"Tell him we still miss him!"

"I'll do that!"

Someone said something unintelligible, and several elves laughed.

"That's right. Hard as we try, no one can carve like he could!"

"I'll tell him that, too!" Beany called.

Grandpa smiled. For a moment he felt warmed. Included. How different from only a few short weeks ago.

He turned his head at the expected tap on the door. "Come in!"

"Hello, Papa Adam. It's Beany!"

"Come in, Beany! How was your day?"

Sounds of footsteps and something heavy being set on the table. "Mine was great, Papa Adam, thanks for asking. But the guys in Santa's personal department had a really rough day."

"Oh?"

"Yeah. I guess there are a lot of problems with the sleigh."

"I've been hearing rumors," Grandpa said.

"Yeah, news travels fast."

"So what's wrong with it?"

"Oh nothing that a big bonfire couldn't cure," Beany said.

Grandpa could hear the smile in the cheerful voice.

"That bad?"

"Well, between you, me, and the mistletoe, I think they should just jack up the reins and put a whole new sleigh under them."

Grandpa laughed. "Sounds pretty drastic."

Beany laughed. "Oh, it is," he said. His voice sobered, "The thing is, I guess they're pretty concerned for the big guy."

"Santa? Is it that bad?"

"Well, the sleigh is pretty old," Beany said. "Older, even, than the man himself."

"Yeah, I guess I knew that," Grandpa said.

"And it really wasn't built to last forever."

"Few things are." Grandpa smiled, rubbing a hand down his frail arm.

"Yeah . . . well . . . they're doing repairs and fixing stuff, but, with every test drive, more things seem to pop up . . . or . . . off."

Grandpa was silent.

"Anyway, my wife is expecting me, so I'd better go before she feeds my dinner to the dog."

Grandpa laughed. "Is that a possibility?"

"Not really," Beany confessed. "Though she certainly does love that dog!" The door closed on his happy laugh.

Grandpa sat, rocking, for a few minutes. Then he got up and took another chair beside the table. He felt around for the cover on his food, lifted it, and sniffed.

"Mmm. Stew! My favorite," he said out loud. He gently explored the tray with his fingers. Fresh bread, still warm. Ooo, crispy, fresh salad! The vegetables must be up!

Happily he settled to his meal, enjoying each bite. He used the bread to scrape at his bowl, trying to sop up each drop of rich broth.

Finally he carefully stacked his used dishes, set them by the door, and moved back to his rocking chair before the fire.

A song began to run through his head. And old song. An old story.

Here comes Santa Claus.
Here comes Santa Claus,
Right down Santa Claus Lane.
Vixen and Blitzen and all his reindeer
Pullin' on the reins.

Grandpa sighed and rocked. He thought about his short visit with Beany.

"Hmmm. What to do. What to do."

Suddenly there was a knock at his door.

Startled, he lifted his head. "Come in!"

Someone clicked the latch and pushed the door open.

"Papa?"

Grandpa's heart stopped for a moment. "Hans?"

His youngest son stepped closer and touched his father's hand. "Yeah, Papa, it's me."

"Hans, it's so good to hear your voice!" Grandpa gripped the offered hand.

"It's been too long, Papa," Hans said.

"Much too long." Grandpa straightened in his chair and cleared his throat. "So what brings you out tonight?" he asked.

"Actually, I just felt like I'd like to talk to you," Hans said. Grandpa heard the scrape of a chair. Then a gasp. "Papa, why are all of your tools spread out on the table?"

"Oh-oh, you've caught me," Grandpa laughed. "I've been playing with my tools!"

Hans snorted softly. "I guess it's your business, Papa," he said apologetically.

"Nothing to it, really," Grandpa said. "I've just started carving again."

There was a moment of silence. "Started . . ." Hans couldn't finish the sentence.

His father laughed. "Yes, son. I've started carving again. Just like you have always been pressing me to."

"And these must be new carvings." Hans was obviously looking around at the packed shelves. "After all of these years," he said softly.

"Well, it takes a long time for an old elf like me to change direction," Grandpa said.

"But ten years, Papa!"

"Well . . . a *very* long time, then."

"So that's what's been going on," Hans said.

"Pardon me?"

"Well, Amy's been over here nearly every day . . ."

"She and I have gotten to be good friends."

"Yes, she can talk about little else," Hans said. Grandpa could hear the smile in his voice. "That and some great secret."

"Well, it really didn't have to be a secret from her parents . . ." Grandpa began.

"Well, it's been good for her," his son said. "She's been so happy and cheerful."

"That sounds like our Amy," Grandpa said, smiling.

"Yes, but it wasn't always so," Hans said.

"What do you mean?"

"Well, I guess it's a normal thing," Hans began.

"Go on."

"Well, you know she's so much younger than our others."

"Twenty years younger," Grandpa put in.

"Yes . . . well . . . we were worried for her. Not having anyone to play with."

"There must be lots of children in the village," Grandpa protested.

"There are a few, but not as many as you would think." He paused. "Huh. I never thought about it before."

"What?"

"That there really aren't very many children in the village."

"So?"

"Oh, nothing. Just a random thought." He paused. "Anyway, back to Amy. We've been worried about her for some time."

"You said that. But why?"

"Well, she has been getting more and more . . . withdrawn," Hans said. "Quiet. Not really . . . happy."

"You're right. That doesn't sound like Amy."

"Anyway, it all seems to be in the past. Now we have our cheerful little girl back, and that's what counts."

"I guess she just needed an interest. Like me," Grandpa said.

"I think you're exactly right," Hans said.

"Can I tell you a little secret now?"

"I'm all ears . . ."

"What?" Grandpa asked.

"I'm listening."

"Well, our little Amy is the one who convinced me to start carving again."

"Amy?"

"Yes. A few weeks ago, she brought me a nice piece of wood. Butternut, if I'm not mistaken."

"And you never are," Hans smiled.

"Anyway, she asked me to carve something for her. I refused, of course."

"Of course," Hans repeated softly.

"But she left the wood with me. And, finally, I . . . just decided to give it a try." He grinned. "The worst I could do was cut off a finger!"

Hans shuddered. "And it went well?"

"Better than well," Grandpa said. "It was almost as though I could see." He sat back in his chair. "I'd nearly forgotten . . ."

"Well, it is so nice that *someone* could finally convince you!"

"I'm sorry, son," Grandpa said. "I know how hard you tried to change my mind." He reached out a gnarled hand, and his son gripped it. "But at least it finally happened."

"And that is the best news I've had since . . . since . . . since the doctor told Carra and I that we were expecting . . . again."

Grandpa laughed. "And if by 'best' you mean 'amazing,' you'd be right." He sobered. "While you're here, son, I'd like to ask you something."

"Ask away."

Grandpa was silent for a moment, gathering his courage. "Why don't you come to see me anymore?"

More silence.

"Hans?"

"I'm almost afraid to tell you, Papa," Hans said.

"Don't be afraid, son."

"Well, it just got so . . . difficult to come here and see you . . . disintegrate before our eyes."

"Disintegrate?"

"Yes. Once you finally gave up on carving, it was as though someone had blown out the candle inside you. Your light just . . . went out."

Grandpa looked thoughtful. "Well," he said slowly, "actually, that is what it was like. Someone taking the light away from me." He grimaced. "And not in the obvious way. It was as though the one thing that kept me alive was gone."

"But *we* were still here, Papa!" Hans said. "We still needed our Papa!"

"All I can say is that I'm sorry, son," Grandpa said. "I guess things happen in their own time."

"You've got that right!" Hans said. "And it's never when we would like them!"

His father smiled. "But now I'm back," he said, "and nothing's ever going to stop my knife again!"

"This is the most wonderful news I've ever had!" Hans said happily. "I can't wait to see the expression on Papa Nels's face when I tell him that your carvings are available again." Grandpa could hear the smile in his son's voice. "He'll flip!"

"Huh. I'd like to see that!" Grandpa said, grinning.

four

Grandpa was just finishing the fine work on the face of a polar bear two mornings later when something hit the roof of his cabin with a loud thump. Startled, he dropped his knife, and almost lost his grip on the bear as well.

Quickly, he ran expert fingers over the model.

"Well," he said philosophically. "I guess you can go through life with one of your canines missing." He set the model on his table and got to his feet, brushing shavings from his lap.

Then he walked to the door and swung it wide open.

A large group of elves had gathered in his front yard. For a moment, he stood there, trying to make out what was being said. No, what was being shouted.

He waved his hands. Finally, the noise died down. He had gotten their attention. "Can anyone tell me what just happened?" he asked.

Several elves started speaking at once. He waved his hands again. "One at a time, please?"

"Papa Adam," Beany's voice spoke from directly in front of him, "we've had a bit of a mishap."

"That I could tell for myself," Grandpa said, his face twisting wryly. "Now, could I have some details?"

"Do any of you guys know what happened?" Beany's voice became muffled. He had obviously turned to someone further away.

"We think all, or at least part, of a runner fell off," another voice responded.

"What? A sleigh runner?" Grandpa asked.

"Well . . . yes, sir," the other voice answered. "It broke loose just after takeoff."

"Not good," Grandpa said.

"No, sir."

For the next few hours, Grandpa's yard was the scene of feverish activity.

A crew was formed to climb up on Grandpa's roof and retrieve the runner. Carefully, they lowered the most important part of Santa's sleigh to the anxiously waiting hands. Then they crawled about on the roof, searching out damage and thumping away busily.

Finally, someone tapped on his door.

"Papa Adam?"

"Come in!" Grandpa called.

His door swung open.

"Just wanted to tell you that we've finished with your roof!"

"Oh, thank you, son," he said. "So does anyone know what happened?"

The elf sighed. "No, but we can guess," he said. "The sleigh just shed one more part."

"I take it this has been happening for some time?"

"It's been getting worse every year," the elf said. "Until this year, though, we never imagined that it could possibly be . . . dangerous."

"And you are concerned for Santa?"

"Of course we are! Whatever would we do if something happened to him?"

"You've got a point," Grandpa said. "Well, let me know if there is anything I can do!"

"Thanks, Papa Adam. But I really don't think there's anything that a *toy carver* could do!" The door closed, and the sounds of his passing faded.

Grandpa smiled and rubbed a gentle thumb over the bear's face. "Nothing a toy carver could do, eh?"

Later that day, when he and Amy were sitting at the table, the litter from two carving projects spread between them, he cleared his throat. "Amy, dear, how would you feel about working on a secret project with me?"

He heard her set her little knife on the table, then her carving. "Oh, Grandpa, I'd love it!" she said enthusiastically. "What are we going to do?" She got up and started toward the cupboard where they stored their pieces of wood.

"You won't find it in there," Grandpa said quietly.

She stopped and came back to him. "Then where, Grandpa?"

"I will need you to take me to the storage sheds," Grandpa said. "But not until after the day-end whistle."

"Mama and Papa will never let me stay that long," Amy protested.

"Oh, let's see if we can convince them," Grandpa said. "Can you be my eyes for a while?"

"I'd love to!" He heard her bounce to her feet. Then his hand was gripped firmly.

"Come on, Grandpa!"

He barely had time to grab his cane before she towed him out the door and onto the sidewalk.

With Amy leading, the trip to her parent's cabin took very little time.

Still, Grandpa was puffing when they reached it.

"Whew!" he said. "You set a real pace, angel!"

She giggled and pushed the front door open. "Mama! Where are you?"

Footsteps came from the kitchen. "What is it, dear? Oh, Papa Adam! What a nice surprise!" The gracious voice with the smile in it greeted him warmly. A soft hand touched his. "It's been far too long since you were here!" The hand took his and led him forward. "Come. Sit a while," she said.

Grandpa lowered himself carefully into the unfamiliar chair. Then he relaxed and smiled. "It *has* been far too long since I was here, Carra," he said warmly. "But that will all change now." He was silent for a moment. "I don't suppose that Hans is around?"

"Before day-end?" Again, Grandpa could hear the smile in her voice. "You taught him too well for that! He'll be here in a few hours." She was quiet for a moment. "Can I convince you to stay and visit? Maybe have supper with us?"

Grandpa smiled. "It would be my pleasure," he said. "I—" but he got no further.

"Papa's home!" Amy sang out.

"What?" Grandpa heard Carra stand up and move away from him. "Well, now I've seen everything!"

The door opened, and Hans came in, breathing heavily. "Everyone saw Papa with Amy, walking down the street!" he gasped out. His voice came closer. "Oh . . . here you are." Grandpa heard the squeak of a chair. "Are you all right, Papa?" Hans asked.

Grandpa smiled. "I'm fine," he said soothingly. "Better than fine."

"Oh, I'm so relieved."

"But what brought you here on the run?"

"Well, it's silly, now that I think about it," Hans said, "but when several elves reported seeing you walking down the street being guided by Amy, for some reason, I panicked, thinking something must have happened and she was trying to get you to safety."

Grandpa laughed. "Well, something did happen a bit earlier today. But not now."

"Yes, I heard about the sleigh runner," Hans said. "I was reassured that you were in no danger, though."

"And that would be correct," Grandpa said. "In fact it was quite exciting."

"I don't understand men," Carra spoke up. "Danger is in no way exciting!"

Both men laughed.

"Also, we are talking about Santa's safety here!"

The laughter ceased.

Grandpa cleared his throat. "Amy? Could you come here, please?"

The little girl crawled up on his lap and snuggled close.

"Now I have to confess something," he said. "Our little darling has been my assistant these past few weeks."

"Yes, we've heard all about how she got you to start carving again," Carra said, the smile back in her voice. "In fact, it's all she will talk about!"

Grandpa smiled. "Well, she has been of more help to me than you will ever know," he said. "And now I must ask for your permission. And your trust."

"What is it, Papa?" Hans asked.

"Well, I have a . . . large project in mind. One that will take many, many weeks. And I was wondering if you would loan me Amy for it."

"Why, of course, Papa Adam," Carra said. "We trust you completely."

"What is your project, Papa?" Hans asked.

"Well, that's where I will need to ask for your trust," Grandpa said. "It is a great secret."

They were silent for a moment.

"I know that you would never do anything that would endanger Amy, Papa Adam," Carra said. "But can't you tell us a little bit more?"

He laughed. "I can tell you that it is a wonderful project and will benefit many, many people."

"But that's all?"

"That's all."

"We'll have to discuss this a bit, Papa Adam," Carra said. "It is a large thing you are asking."

"I know," Grandpa agreed. "But, like I say, it will be something very, very good."

"Would you excuse us for a moment?"

"Certainly, Hans."

Amy's parents stood up and moved into the next room. Grandpa could hear the murmur of their voices.

Amy turned in his lap. "So what are we going to do, Grandpa?" she asked.

He put a finger to his lips. "Shhh. It's a great secret!"

She giggled and snuggled closer.

Hans and Carra returned, taking chairs on either side of Grandpa.

"We'd be happy to loan you Amy," Hans said. "As long as you don't tire her out too much!"

"Oh, thank you," Grandpa said, holding out his hand. "This means a lot to me."

"And to me!" Amy piped in.

Everyone laughed.

Supper that evening was a renewal. Of family. Of affection. Of ties too long left slack.

It was a wonderful evening.

A perfect evening.

But to someone who, until recently, had spent most of his time in the close confines of his tiny cabin, it was also very tiring. By the time Amy and her father had left Grandpa at his front door, he was almost too weary to climb to his bedroom on the second floor. He dropped into bed without even removing his boots.

five

Grandpa spent the morning cleaning out the little shed behind his cabin. It had been some time since anyone had set foot in it, and there was a deep layer of dust covering everything.

He enlisted the help of Beany for the heavy work.

"What about these big cargo doors?" Beany asked after he finished oiling the hinges on the front door.

"Oil them too," Grandpa said. "You never know when I might need them!"

Beany shook his head. "Never saw a carving that big!" he said, almost under his breath.

Grandpa just smiled.

Finally the two of them stood back.

"So, how does it look?" Grandpa asked.

"Clean," Beany said promptly. "But tell me, Papa Adam, why are we doing this?"

"I am getting tired of having to clean up shavings in the cabin," Grandpa told him. "It just makes sense to move my mess out here to the shed, where it belongs."

"I guess," Beany said slowly. "And you'll have more room in here, too."

"There is that," Grandpa agreed.

"But isn't it . . . rather drafty?"

"Oh, I'll keep a fire burning," Grandpa reassured him. "I used to work out here all the time before . . ."

"Before you stopped carving," Beany put in. "But, Papa Adam, that was years ago!"

Grandpa laughed. "That it was, Beany," he said. "But I'm just as hardy now as I was then. I'll survive!"

"I guess," Beany said halfheartedly.

"Well, thank you for your help!" Grandpa said, holding out his hand.

Beany took it carefully. "Um . . . you're welcome, Papa Adam," he said.

The lunch whistle sounded.

"Good timing!" Beany laughed. "I'll run and get your lunch!"

Late that afternoon, Grandpa and Amy were, once again, facing each other across a table. This time, in the little shed. Grandpa was carving, Amy buffing.

"There, Grandpa," Amy said. "I think I'm finished!"

Grandpa put down his carving and reached out. She carefully pushed the delicate figure of a bird into his questing fingers.

"Ah. Yes, it feels very good," he said, running expert fingers over the smooth sides. "Oh . . . here's a spot."

Amy took the bird back and carefully examined it. "Wow, you found that?" she asked. "I totally missed it. It's no bigger than a speck." She giggled. "Grandpa, your eyes are better than mine!"

Grandpa smiled. "Never thought I'd hear that again," he said, almost to himself. He leaned back in his chair and tipped his head to one side as a whistle blew outside. "Ah. Day-end."

Amy set her bird down carefully. "So are we going?" she asked.

"In a few minutes," Grandpa told her. "Let's wait a while for everyone to leave."

They continued to work. Finally, Grandpa put his carving down once more and got to his feet. "I think it's time now," he said.

Amy jumped eagerly to her feet and bounced to the door. "Come on, Grandpa!" she said.

Grandpa grabbed his cane and joined her.

She pulled him eagerly down the steps toward the street.

"Hold on a moment, angel!" he said, laughing. "We'll need something to help us carry the wood back." He freed himself and, using his cane to direct himself, walked around the side of his cabin. He emerged a short time later, pulling a small, heavy wagon that protested loudly with each revolution of the wheels.

"What are we going to do with that?" Amy asked.

"It's going to hold our wood," Grandpa said. "Big pieces are very heavy, and you and I won't be able to carry them."

"Oh. Okay!" Amy said cheerfully. "Come on, Grandpa!"

The trip to the storage sheds took only a couple of minutes. Amy paused in the entrance of the huge, barnlike building. "Wow, it's awfully dark in there," she said.

Grandpa laughed. "Welcome to my world!" he said cheerfully. He sniffed the air. Basswood. Evergreen. Oak. Beech. Ash. Maple. Even some exotic ebony. He smiled. The smells were at once familiar and welcoming. "Come on, dear," he said, moving forward.

This time, it was Grandpa who led. Amy hung back slightly, fearful of the dim light and dark shadows here in this enormous structure.

"I'm a little scared, Grandpa," she admitted. "Usually when I come here, there are lanterns and lots of elves."

"You don't have to be scared, darling," he told her. "There's just wood here. Different kinds of wood. Warm, friendly wood."

"I guess so," she said hesitantly.

"Come on, angel. I'll protect you!"

Amy giggled halfheartedly.

"Now, I need you to point out the larger pieces," Grandpa said.

She was quiet, but he could feel her moving as she looked right and left.

"There's only small bits in this room," she said. "This is where I found all of the pieces we've been using."

"Ah. Right," he said. "Well, let's see what's in the next room."

The two of them made their way slowly, carefully past the stacks and through the nearest doorway.

"Oh, these are much bigger!" Amy exclaimed, forgetting her anxiety.

"Lead me to them," Grandpa said.

Amy pulled on his arm, then directed his hand toward the nearest of the large pieces. He ran his hands over several.

"Yes, these are nearly big enough," he said. "Let's see what's in the next room."

Again, Amy led him deeper into the large wood shed. "Gee, Grandpa, it's really dark in here!"

"Can you see enough to lead me around?"

"I guess so." The little voice sounded doubtful.

"If it is going to be dangerous, I don't want you to do it," Grandpa said.

"It's getting better now," Amy said.

"Getting used to the dimness?"

"I guess so. I can see better, anyway."

"So what do you see?"

"Well, there are lots and lots of big tree trunks stored here," she said, "cut into pieces."

"Lead on."

Amy towed him over to the right and stopped. He reached down, encountering rough bark. "Ah. Oak," he said. He shook his head. "Not what I was looking for."

Amy led him to another corner of the vast room.

"Yes. This is just the thing," he said, running sensitive fingers along the length of another tree. He sniffed. "Mmm, beech."

"Will this do, Grandpa?"

"Perfectly," Grandpa said. "But now, we will need our wagon."

"I'll get it!" Amy cried. He could hear her little footsteps move away. A short time later, she was back, accompanied by the tell-tale squeak of the heavy wagon.

"Pull it over here," Grandpa said, indicating. "There."

"Okay, now we're going to roll this wood onto the cart," Grandpa said. "First, we have to block the wheels." He showed Amy how to jam small pieces of wood under the wheels. "There, that will keep it from moving."

Together they managed to roll several of the slices of log onto their cart.

"There. That should keep us out of mischief for a while," Grandpa said cheerfully. "Let's go."

Carefully, with Amy leading, the two of them maneuvered the cart back through the crowded shed and out into the evening air.

"It's sure nice to get out here into the light again," Amy said.

"Yes, I suppose it is," Grandpa agreed quietly.

"What's the matter, Grandpa?"

"Nothing. Nothing, dear. Just . . . feeling a little sorry for myself. It'll pass."

"Oh. Ummm . . . okay." Amy sounded uncertain.

"So is there anyone out?" Grandpa asked, his cheerful tone restored.

"Not that I can see," Amy answered promptly.

"Good. Because this is supposed to be a secret, remember?"

"I remember." She skipped ahead. "This is fun, Grandpa!"

"Except when my guide leaves me," Grandpa laughed.

"Oh. Sorry!" She skipped back and put her hand over the large gnarled one pulling the cart. "We're almost there."

"Good. I'm getting tired," Grandpa said.

"Here's your cabin," Amy said. "Now what do we do?"

"Help me push this cart around to the back," Grandpa said.

With a minimum of effort and a maximum of grunting, the two of them managed to negotiate Grandpa's yard and wedge the cart against the small step leading to the shed.

"Now we roll the slices onto the step and into the shed," Grandpa instructed.

Soon, they were standing in the shed, surrounded by large pieces of beech tree.

Grandpa smiled. "And now the work starts on Santa's new sleigh."

six

The work was painfully slow. Choosing the woods—something he turned over almost exclusively to Amy—and then hauling them, turned out to be the easiest part of the whole process. Cutting and laminating took an excruciating amount of time. Though he had performed similar tasks in the past, this was the first time Grandpa was doing everything without the aid of his eyes. Amy was invaluable when it came to matching patterns, but for the physical work, Grandpa had only himself.

But as he labored steadily on, he began to notice . . . changes. More energy, for one. An increase in stamina. When he finished working for the day, he no longer fell into his bed, completely exhausted.

Now he was able to sit up and plan the work for the next day, check up on the setting of seams, and other things.

Another change was brought to his attention forcibly as he opened the door to the shed one morning.

He had completely forgotten his cane. That same cane that had been his constant companion these past several years, and without which he hadn't been able to stand, let alone walk.

That cane. Which was now somewhere in his cabin. Without him.

His smile that day could have lit the entire North Pole.

Almost as bright as the day he was finally finished with the preparation work and was able to start carving.

Throughout this time of feverish activity, he was very conscious of the many and various accidents to Santa's current sleigh, kept constantly up-to-date by Amy, her parents, and the gregarious Beany.

The tension was rising throughout the entire community. Santa's safety was something that concerned everyone.

A team of carpenters were crawling over and through every part of the old sleigh, reinforcing, adjusting, replacing. And still the mishaps went on.

Two elves had been injured during a test drive, one seriously. And it was getting more and more difficult to find volunteer reindeer. The older, more experienced fliers were flatly refusing to go up with "the wreck," as they were calling the old sleigh. And now the elves had taken to searching out the younger and more foolhardy in the herds, just to keep the testing going.

"But that's just crazy!" Grandpa said when Beany filled him in on the latest news.

"Papa Nels was telling some elves this morning that the head of Santa's personal department went with the chief herder to choose volunteers himself," Beany said.

"Those young bulls? They haven't got an ounce of sense between them!" Grandpa laid down the knife he was using and searched carefully through his neatly arranged tools for something else.

"But it's true," Amy protested from her seat at the table. She flicked some shavings away and lifted her carving to the light. "Papa saw them walking out to the fields this morning."

"This just keeps getting worse and worse," Grandpa said under his breath. He found what he was looking for and started scraping at the large piece he was carving.

"Well, it is what it is," Beany said. He set the tray he was carrying on the table, and Grandpa heard his heavy footsteps move toward the door. "I have to be getting back," he said. His footsteps stopped. "What are you working on now, Papa Adam?" he asked.

"It's a . . ." Amy began.

"It's a new toy," Grandpa said, forestalling her. "Adult-sized."

"Oh. Well, that should be nice," Beany said. He stepped outside and swung the door shut behind him.

"I wasn't going to tell him, Grandpa!" Amy protested when Beany's heavy footsteps had faded away.

"I'm sorry, dear. I wasn't sure what you were going to say," Grandpa said.

"I was going to tell him that it was a new design," she said.

Grandpa laughed. "Which was probably a better lie than the one I came up with!"

"It *wasn't* a lie," she protested. "It was the truth. You *are* working on a new design."

Grandpa was silent for a moment. "Huh. You're right," he said with a smile. "Again, you've proved that you're smarter than your old grandpa!"

Amy giggled.

The two of them worked for a few minutes in silence.

"So how is it going, Grandpa?" Amy asked, finally. "The sleigh, I mean."

"Well . . . slowly," Grandpa said.

"Is it going to be done in time for Christmas?"

Grandpa was silent for a moment.

"Grandpa?"

"I'm not sure, angel," he said. "It's coming, but not as quickly as I would have hoped. I have most of the dash done. But I'm just starting on the runners and I still have the sides and the rear to form."

"Can I help?"

"Well, I've been giving that some thought," Grandpa said. "I was wondering if you would be able to work on the runners."

"I can do it, Grandpa!" Amy said excitedly.

"Well, I have been thinking about how you could," he said slowly. "We'd have to brace things so you wouldn't have to hold it by yourself."

"But—" she started.

"A runner would be far heavier than the little pieces of wood you have been working with," he added over her protest.

Amy was quiet for a few minutes, absorbing that. "Could we try?" she asked finally, in a small voice.

"Yes, let's," Grandpa said, smiling. He got to his feet and began gathering braces and clamps. "Now our problem is trying to hold everything so you can carve." He carried one of the long runners to the table and set it down. "As you can see, I've got it roughly formed. All that's left to do is the 'pretty' stuff."

Amy giggled. "That's the part I like the best!" she said.

"Don't we all!"

Grandpa began to devise a system of clamps and braces, finally getting the unwieldy piece firmly fastened to the table and in a position for Amy to go to work.

"There, angel. What do you think?"

Amy moved slowly forward, finally getting close enough to touch.

"It's perfect, Grandpa!" she said. "Do you know what you want?"

Grandpa was silent. "I don't," he said at last.

Amy was quiet for a few seconds.

"Do you?" Grandpa asked.

"Shhh! I'm talking to it," Amy said.

"Ummm . . . okay," Grandpa said, smiling. He walked back to the dashboard and sat down. "Let me know what it's thinking."

Amy giggled. "I can't," she said, "it's a great secret!"

Grandpa laughed.

Through the next few weeks, Grandpa kept a surreptitious "eye" on Amy's progress. As soon as she left for the day, he would run expert fingers over her day's carving. He was quite astonished at what she had been able to accomplish. And the level of workmanship.

"Little elflet is better than me," he muttered.

It soon became obvious the she was carving the heavy runners to look like clouds.

Grandpa frowned. "Huh. I guess I should have talked to her about 'drag' and 'lift.'" He sighed. "Well, we'll just have to hope that good old North Pole magic can make up for any lack on our part!"

Slowly the sleigh began to take shape. The gently curved dash, with its North Pole scenes, was finally attached to one of the sides, which continued the North Pole theme with visions of flying reindeer. That, in turn, was fixed to the rear end, which was carved into Christmas scenes. Images of happy children giving and receiving gifts in the holiday spirit.

It was finally beginning to resemble a sleigh. So much so that they had to forestall Beany when he brought their meals. Now they would greet him from Grandpa's front porch and take their meals in the cabin.

Grandpa was becoming quite hopeful that they would soon be able to finish.

Amy's work on the runners was no less amazing. The pair of them stood, ready to be attached, in a corner of the shop. And Amy soon proved that she was not only capable of expert carving, but also that she was able to surprise even her grandfather, the best carver in the whole community.

She had been carving something else. Something she wouldn't let her grandfather "see." Then, one afternoon, she brought it to him.

"It's ready, Grandpa," she said happily, "but I don't know how to attach it."

"What is it you have been working on so secretly?" Grandpa asked, reaching out.

Amy pressed something into the gnarled hands. "This," she said simply.

"And what is 'this'?" Grandpa smiled. He ran sensitive fingers gently over her carving. "Huh. What *is* this?"

"It's an extra piece for the runner," Amy said. "I just thought that it needed a piece out to the side. You know, like a bird's wing?"

Grandpa was silent, running his fingers again and again over the carving. He knew what it was now.

A wing. A wing made of clouds. He smiled. Genius! And from a five-year-old! He reached out and Amy moved closer, ducking her head under the gentle hand.

"This is perfect, angel," he said.

Amy giggled. "Will it work, Grandpa?" she asked.

"It will. Beautifully," he told her. "I'm so proud of you!"

She giggled again. "The runners just . . . 'spoke' to me," she said. "I just knew when I looked at them what they needed."

"I think there will be a day, not too distant, when I will know that my youngest grandchild has surpassed me," Grandpa said softly, pulling her close in a warm hug.

"Sur-passed?"

"Become a better carver than her grandpa."

"Oh. I could never be that, Grandpa," she said. "You're the best!"

"But that's how it's supposed to be, honey," Grandpa said. "The teacher teaches. The student learns. Then the student passes the teacher and becomes the next teacher."

"Grandpa, I couldn't teach!" She giggled. "I'm too little!"

"You won't be too little forever," Grandpa said. "And besides," he held out her carving, "this isn't the work of a student."

"What? Yes it is! *I* made it!"

"Well, it's proof that the student has already passed the teacher."

"Grandpa, you say funny things!" Amy giggled.

"Well, anyway, let's see how we can attach it, shall we?" Grandpa got to his feet and set her carving on the table. Then he dragged one of the runners over.

For the rest of the day, the two of them drilled holes, applied glue, and tamped pegs. Finally Grandpa ran his hands over their finished product.

"Perfect," he said. "Absolutely perfect!"

The left runner now had a horizontal piece, which protruded seamlessly to the outside, providing both lift and stability to the whole sleigh.

Grandpa smiled at Amy. "This will solve all the problems I have been struggling with in my old brain," he said, blinking rapidly.

"Good," Amy said, satisfied. "I'll get started on the other one. Uh-oh. Day-end whistle, Grandpa. We'd better get going."

"You go, dear, and meet Beany," Grandpa said softly. "I've something to do first."

"Okeydokey!" she sang out.

The door slammed.

Grandpa allowed the tears to come. He sank to his knees in the soft shavings that thoroughly littered the wood floor, heedless of the wet tracks down his cheeks and of the droplets that fell.

"Father Creator?" he whispered. "Thank you for that very special little girl." He shook his head, spattering tears. "I don't know where I'd be if you hadn't sent her to me." He sat back on his heels. "No, I do know where I'd be," he said. "I'd still be sitting on my porch, barely able to get around, and waiting for something . . . anything . . . to break up my long, useless days." He tipped his head back, turning sightless eyes toward heaven. "I cannot sufficiently express my gratitude," he went on, his voice a mere thread of sound. "Thank you. Thank you. Thank you."

He got to his feet and went to join his very special little granddaughter for supper.

seven

The sleigh was nearly finished. Amy's other modified runner had been installed, and she and Grandpa were now working on the seats, crafted from the finest leather and stuffed with the very softest of pure white wool.

But as consumed as he was by what they were doing, Grandpa was also conscious of the feverish activity going on all around them.

Final preparations were being completed for Santa's annual run. Toys inspected and packed for the all-important delivery. Last-minute letters examined and wishes documented and addressed.

And hanging over everything, the gnawing uncertainty and doubt surrounding Santa's aged sleigh.

And his safety.

Beany was an excellent source of information in these last, frantic days.

"And so they've decided to bring in this expert," he said.

"An expert? Now? At this late date?" Grandpa shook his head. "There are only four more days till Christmas Eve!"

"Well, yeah." Beany shrugged. "I guess they figure that it's better to be late than dead."

Grandpa shivered and continued with his careful stitching. Amy was across the room, carding wool.

"So what are you two doing, now?" Beany changed the subject.

"Stuffing," Amy said promptly.

"More toys," Grandpa said.

"Ah. Well, I'd better be going," Beany said. "Do you have anything else to send for packing?"

Grandpa had been sending the toys he and Amy had carved earlier, in small batches, further disguising their present project.

Grandpa carefully set down the piece of soft leather he had been sewing and crossed the room to retrieve a small, wooden box. "I think this is the rest of it," he said, handing the box to Beany.

Beany peeked inside. "Oh, these are wonderful!" he said, lifting a small, delicate toy airplane. "Forgive me, Papa Adam, when I say that these are just as good as what you used to carve!"

"No need to ask forgiveness," Grandpa said, smiling. "That is probably the best thing you could tell me!"

Beany grinned. "Well, that's good then." He closed the door firmly behind him.

Amy crossed to the window as Beany's heavy boots clomped down the front steps. "It sure is snowing, Grandpa," she said. "It's getting deeper and deeper!"

"About time too," Grandpa said. "We were getting a bit worried. Four days before Christmas is rather late to be getting our first snow at the North Pole!"

Amy giggled. "I know," she said. "Usually Papa is able to come sledding with me lots of times before Christmas."

"You and your Papa go sledding, do you?"

"It's our favorite thing," Amy said, returning to her heap of wool. "We're going as soon as he gets home from work tonight."

"Oh, that'll be fun," Grandpa said. He picked up his leather and began stitching once more. "I used to go with your Papa when he was your age."

"He told me," Amy said. "It was his favorite thing then too."

Grandpa laughed. "He was certainly enthusiastic about it," he said. "I was very happy to have something special between us."

"Because he was *your* baby? Like I'm *his* baby?"

"Exactly. There were three boys older than him," Grandpa said. "Easy to get lost in the shuffle."

"Shuffle?"

"Figure of speech, angel. It means that sometimes it's hard for the littlest one to get noticed."

"Ooooh. I know what that means," Amy said, giggling. "When my brothers come to visit, with all of their kids, no one notices me."

"Don't you believe it," Grandpa said. "Everyone notices you!"

Amy giggled again. "Well, it seems like they're all spending time looking after the other kids," she said.

"Well, the little ones *need* looking after," Grandpa told her. "They can't do it for themselves. But don't think for one minute that no one is noticing you just because they don't have to change your swadding anymore or feed you with a bottle."

"Grandpa! Yuck! Change my swadding?"

"Well, you know what I mean."

"Yeah, I guess I do."

Grandpa stood up. "Well this piece is done," he said. "How is the carding coming?"

The two of them spent the rest of the afternoon installing and stuffing the seat.

Grandpa ran his hands over the finished product. "Feels pretty good," he said.

Amy climbed up and sat down. "Oooo, Grandpa! Come and sit beside me!"

Grandpa climbed up and perched gingerly on the soft leather. "Mmmm. It is rather nice," he said, smoothing his hands over the seat on both sides of him.

"Rather nice?" Amy exclaimed indignantly. "It feels like we're sitting on a cloud!"

"Which is probably a good thing," Grandpa said. "Poor Santa has to spend a lot of time sitting on it!"

Amy giggled again. "So, Grandpa, when are we going to give it to Santa?"

"I think tomorrow will be plenty soon enough," he said thoughtfully. "That will give them time to start the loading."

"Goody! I can't wait to see the look on Santa's face!"

"Me neither." Grandpa grinned.

"Grandpa, you're so funny!" Small arms were thrown around him. "I love you, Grandpa!"

"And I love you too, darling," Grandpa said, returning the hug. "More than you will ever know!"

The little girl slid from the seat and headed for the door. "See you tomorrow!" she sang out.

"Oh, wait a moment, dear!" Grandpa said, climbing down from the sleigh. "I need one more favor from you before you leave today."

"Okeydokey," the little girl said, stopping just inside the door and turning toward him. "What do you need, Grandpa?"

"I want you to take me down to the stables."

"The stables? But it's dark outside. Why do you want to go there?"

"Well, I need to have a little chat with Dasher."

"Really?"

"We used to be fast friends," Grandpa said. "I need to talk to him about tomorrow's presentation."

"Oh. Well, okay. Come on, Grandpa. I've got to hurry. Papa's taking me sledding, remember?"

"I do," Grandpa said, reaching for his coat. "You just have to take me there," he said. "I can get someone else to help me home."

"Okeydokey!"

The walkways had been shoveled right to the stable door, so Grandpa had no trouble negotiating along the way.

Amy dropped his hand once he had the stable door open. "Well, see you tomorrow, Grandpa!" she said.

"Thanks, darling!"

She was gone.

Grandpa stopped in the doorway of the stable and sniffed. Alfalfa hay and clean wheat straw.

"Almost as good as the smell in a wood shop," he said softly.

A loud snort was his only answer.

"Dasher? Is that you?"

Hoofs clopping on the hard-packed floor. Then a nudge. Grandpa reached out with gentle fingers, touching the velvet softness of the large, warm nose.

"How are you, old friend?" he asked.

Another nudge.

"I know I haven't been to see you in a little while."

A loud snort.

"Okay, okay in a long while." Grandpa laughed. "But things have been . . . difficult for me."

Another nudge. And the gentle touch of a tongue on his hand.

"Well, it's all behind me, now," he went on. "Thanks to Amy, I'm carving again."

A deep breath of relief.

"I feel the same way, old friend," he said, rubbing the nose once more. "I was pretty far gone."

Another nudge. Then Grandpa felt a large, warm body move close against him. He put one arm over the bony shoulders.

"I know I had you, my friend," he said, "but sometimes, someone just has to be hit over the head before they're willing to make any changes."

The large body bumped into him, almost knocking him off his feet.

"Exactly," he chuckled. "And thank you."

Another bump.

"But the main reason I'm here tonight is concerning Santa's sleigh."

The reindeer moved away from him slightly and snorted.

"I know. I've heard about it," Grandpa said. "I think I might have a solution. But I need your help first."

Another snort. The body moved closer again.

"Could you come with me to my place?"

The large body moved instantly toward the front door.

"Umm. I take it the answer is yes." Grandpa laughed. "Could you wait for me, big guy?"

The reindeer set a fast pace back to Grandpa's cabin. Grandpa led the way around the side to his shed.

"Is anyone around?" he asked.

The reindeer was silent for a moment, then shoved Grandpa toward the door with a gentle nose.

"Okay, come on in."

Grandpa stood back to allow room for the large animal to navigate.

Dasher stopped just inside the door.

"So. What do you think?"

Grandpa was unprepared for the large animal's response. The old elf was thrust back against the door by one large swipe of a very rough, very enthusiastic tongue.

He scrubbed at his cheek, laughing. "So you think it will do?"

Another swipe.

"Ugh! Dasher! Stop it!"

Another swipe.

"Okay, okay, I get it!"

The animal moved away from him and made a slow circuit of the sleigh. Finally he returned to Grandpa, who had remained close to the door. The old elf could feel the enthusiastic approval radiating from the shaggy beast.

"Good," he said simply. "I was hoping you'd like it!" He held up a hand. "Stop!" The rough tongue halted near his face. Grandpa pushed at the large head and laughed. "We're going to have to find a better way for you to show approval," he said. Then he sobered. "But now I have one more problem to overcome before I can present this to Santa."

He felt the large animal turn away from him, looking toward the sleigh. Dasher lifted his two front feet and stomped them on the floor.

"Right, my friend. We need to take it for a test run."

The reindeer turned back to him, shoved him toward his chair, and disappeared through the door in a flurry of hoof beats.

Grandpa laughed and closed the door. Then he walked over to the chair and sat down to wait.

eight

He didn't wait long. A thump on his door brought him out of a light doze.

He crossed to the door, swung it wide, and sniffed. "Smells like reindeer." He grinned.

A soft nose touched his hand. He reached out to smooth his fingers down a long, furry face. "Feels like reindeer too," he added. "So how many of you are there?"

Dasher nudged his hand again. Eight times.

"All of you?"

A snort.

"How did you manage that?"

Shuffle of feet.

"Okay, keep your secret." Grandpa laughed.

Dasher nudged him gently and moved closer, jingling a little.

"What?" Grandpa's questing hands encountered a harness. An expertly applied harness. "How on earth did you convince someone to harness you?" he asked.

Another snort. Somehow sounding . . . disgusted.

"Of course. What was I thinking! Your every whim is immediately addressed!" Grandpa laughed. "But how do you keep them from asking questions? Or at least getting curious?"

This time, Dasher thumped Grandpa in the chest.

"Okay . . . okay, I get it!" Grandpa gasped. "You are the kings here!"

The large head beside him moved up and down emphatically.

"So should we get started?"

It was fortunate that all of the reindeer knew exactly where they were to stand and at least the basics of harnessing, because Grandpa would have been lost in seconds, trying to *feel* his way through the unfamiliar process.

Finally, he stepped back. "All right?" he asked.

Dasher, the near side leader, shook himself, jingling his harness. Then he nudged Grandpa and nodded his head.

Grandpa moved to the seldom-used cargo doors. "Sure you're ready for this?" he asked.

The sound of eight fully grown reindeer shaking their harnesses.

Grandpa laughed. "I'll take that as a 'yes,' " he said, swinging the heavy doors wide on noiseless hinges.

"Hello, Grandpa!" Amy's little voice sang out.

Grandpa grabbed onto the door. "Amy, darling, you nearly gave me a heart attack!" he gasped.

"Sorry!" Amy rushed to his side. "Are you all right?"

"I will be," he said, finally managing a smile. "Just don't give your old Grandpa too many surprises like that!"

Her little arms went around him. "I won't, Grandpa. I promise," she whispered. She moved, turning her head. "So am I right?' she asked. "Is the big test tonight?"

"How did you know that?" Grandpa demanded, asking and answering her question at the same time.

"I just knew!" Amy said. He could hear the smile in her voice.

"I guess you know your Grandpa a little too well," Grandpa said.

"I guess I do." Amy giggled as she moved away from him. "Let's go!" she said.

"Amy, dear, I don't think you should." Grandpa reached for her. "It might be dangerous."

A small snort. "Like anything you made would be junk!" she scoffed softly. "Come on, Grandpa. I'm already inside!"

"Hold on, while I get in!" Grandpa called out. He tumbled unceremoniously into the front seat.

"Oof!" Amy said. "Maybe I'd better sit over here!" She slid to the right.

Grandpa grinned and grabbed for the loose reins, untangling them and looping them around a short, wooden staff, carved just for that purpose. Then he lowered a delicately carved wooden bar across their knees and fastened it into its bracket. "Okay, we're rea—hey!"

They were off. In two leaps, the reindeer were in the air, pulling on the new sleigh with all the enthusiasm they had habitually given the old one—before it had become a death trap. The sleigh, so ungainly on the ground, bounded lightly into the air behind the reindeer.

"Oh, my—!" Grandpa swallowed the rest of what he had been going to say as he was flung back into the seat. He threw one arm around his little grand-daughter and grabbed onto the dash with the desperate fingers of his other hand.

The reindeer made a careful "off" turn, straightened for a few seconds, then tried an equally cautious "near" turn. The sleigh responded perfectly. They began to ascend, slowly, carefully. Then more abruptly. Using sharper movements.

The sleigh followed their every move.

Suddenly, Blitzen, in the off-wheeler position closest to Grandpa, snorted loudly.

That was Grandpa's only warning as the sleigh began a series of erratic movements. Movements designed to test and try it.

Or to shake Grandpa out of his suspenders.

And still the sleigh followed unerringly.

Dasher finally straightened out and banked into a slow off turn, once more, headed for home.

"So are we done?" Grandpa asked, rather breathlessly. "Because if we are—"

He never got a chance to finish. The sleigh suddenly veered sharply, leaving him with the feeling that he had just abandoned something important in the air behind them.

"Hey, what the—?" someone shouted.

"It's another sleigh, Grandpa!" Amy shouted. "Santa's old one!"

"Oh, fantastic," Grandpa muttered.

"The young bulls pulling it don't know what to do!" Amy screamed. "They're all trying to fly away! They're not pulling together!"

Grandpa could picture the scene. Young, completely untrained reindeer. Every bull for himself. It was a nightmare.

Dasher guided his team in a quick near turn. The experienced members flew together perfectly, as one. Their movements smooth and sure. Grandpa and Amy hardly suffered a bump through the entire procedure.

But Grandpa knew it wasn't the same story in the other sleigh.

And he was right. His heightened hearing soon picked up the sound he had been dreading. The sudden, sharp noise of wood cracking.

"What is it, Amy!" he shouted.

"It's the main piece that connects the team to the sleigh, Grandpa!"

Grandpa's heart stopped. The main tree. "Dasher!" Grandpa shouted. "They're in trouble!"

But Dasher had already seen and was guiding his team closer.

"I think the driver knows something's wrong," Amy said. "He's throwing stuff out."

"What stuff?"

"Blankets, tool boxes. Anything he can grab, it looks like." She paused. "He sees us! He sees us! Reach out your hands, Grandpa! He's trying to grab us!"

Grandpa leaned over the side and stuck his hands out, blindly. He felt someone grip his wrists tightly. And then Dasher was swerving away.

"You got him, Grandpa. You got him!" Amy sang out.

Grandpa felt as though his arms were slowly being pulled from their sockets. For several very tense seconds, the other elf hung from his frail wrists. Then, with relief, Grandpa felt the runners touch down.

The strong hands released him as the other elf dropped to the ground.

For several seconds, Grandpa sat there, rubbing his strained arms and wrists. Then he got shakily to his feet and stepped out of the sleigh.

"Are you there?" he asked.

"I am!' someone at his feet gasped. "I'm here. Thanks to you!"

"I'm glad," Grandpa said simply. "Ummm . . . who are you?"

"He's the elf they brought in to test Santa's sleigh!" Amy said excitedly. "He was talking to Papa this morning!"

"That's right," the other elf said, getting to his feet. Finally, his voice had reached a level just above Grandpa's own. Then Grandpa felt his hand gripped firmly. "Thank you!" the elf said fervently.

"You're welcome," Grandpa said, smiling. "Sooo . . . what happened?"

"It was a nightmare," the elf began. "Oh, by the way, I'm Owen."

"Nice to meet you, Owen," Grandpa said, offering his hand once more.

"And I'm especially glad to meet you . . . ?" Owen waited.

"Oh, I'm Adam," Grandpa said.

"Everyone calls him Papa Adam," Amy put in, " 'cause he's so old!"

Grandpa grimaced. "Thank you, Amy," he said.

"Welcome!"

"Anyway, to get back to the story," Owen said, "I was testing that foul contraption that someone dares to call a sleigh, when *my* team . . . met . . . *your* team."

"I guess we needn't discuss which team was the most experienced." Grandpa smiled.

"Indeed," Owen said. "It's my understanding that the more qualified reindeer refused to pull the old sleigh." He laughed shakily. "Now I know why!" He sighed. "Anyway, we were doing all right, until we met you."

"I deeply regret that," Grandpa said. "If we'd known anyone else was out . . ."

"You needn't apologize," Owen said. "If it hadn't taken me so long to patch things together . . . If I'd had a proper team . . . If the sleigh wasn't a piece of junk . . . If . . . if . . . if . . ."

"You're right. Too many 'ifs.'" Grandpa grinned.

"When my team veered away, the tree cracked almost through. I tried to lighten the load . . ."

"I can only imagine what the countryside thought when blankets and tools started raining down on their heads!" Grandpa laughed.

"They must have thought it was some sort of macabre hail storm!" Owen agreed. "Anyway, it might have bought me a bit of time, but the sleigh itself was doomed. If you hadn't come along when you did, I'd be down on the ground with it!"

"I take it that the sleigh and its team didn't arrive together?"

"It would be a sorry tale for the reindeer if they had," Owen said. "No, the tree broke a second after I grabbed your wrists and, luckily for the reindeer, the traces pulled right out of the rotten cross tree. The entire sleigh fell to the ground." Another sigh. "It's probably just a heap of matchsticks now."

"Well, then it'll be useful once more!" Grandpa laughed.

"The only sad thing is that I don't know what Santa will do now," Owen said sadly.

"Well, I might have a solution—" Grandpa began.

"Owen are you all right?" another voice had joined them.

"I'm fine. I'm fine!" Owen reassured them.

"Owen!" another voice. Then a babble of voices, overlapping each other. "Owen, we saw the sleigh fall . . ."

". . . thought you were a goner . . ."

" . . . couldn't imagine how you could survive . . ."

" . . . terrible!"

Owen laughed. "Hey!" Silence descended. "I'm fine, everyone! See?"

Murmurings. Threatening to break out into another babble.

"Really! I'm fine!"

Someone, puffing heavily, joined them. "The team is okay!" he shouted. "They landed just over there. They're a bit shaken up but okay!"

"And the sleigh landed over in that direction," someone else came up, also breathing noisily. "I'm afraid it's gone for good."

There was a short silence at his words.

Then someone asked. "Where did this sleigh come from?"

nine

* * ❅ ❆ ❋ ❄ * ₊ *

Grandpa, everyone is looking at our sleigh," Amy whispered.

Grandpa shrugged. "Well, I guess it was bound to happen," he said. "Our secret appears to be out!"

"We made it," Amy said loudly. "Grandpa and me."

"What?" someone gasped.

"Grandpa and me. We made the sleigh. Carved it," Amy said. "From beech wood."

"You? And Papa Adam?"

Grandpa could hear the disbelief in the voice. He cleared his throat. "It's true," he said. He reached out, and Amy moved under his arm. "Amy and I have been working on it for months. In my shop."

Silence.

"Forgive us, Papa Adam," another elf said, "but I, for one, am having a hard time believing that you with your . . . disability and . . ."

"And Amy," Grandpa supplied.

" . . . a small child could . . . do . . . something like this."

Grandpa laughed. It sounded a bit strained but was still serviceable. "So you're suggesting my blindness and her age are a . . . handicap?"

"No! Well . . . yes," the elf said.

This time, Grandpa's laugh sounded real. "I'm sorry to have to differ with you, but the fact remains, Amy and I carved this sleigh. Together. For Santa." He smiled. "And, between you and me, Amy doesn't think we're handicapped. To quote her and her papa, all you really need are hands. And heart."

A low murmur of disbelief.

"But for now, the only *fact* you need is this—we made this sleigh. If you need another voice, ask the reindeer," Grandpa said, waving a hand.

"Hey, that's Santa's team!" Someone had just noticed the reindeer hitched to the new sleigh.

"Ask them," Grandpa said again.

"Hey, Dasher! Any truth to Papa Adam's claims?"

A low grunt from the lead reindeer. Then from each of the reindeer. Then a final shake and jangle of harness.

"I guess they're telling the truth," said a disbelieving voice.

"What's going on here?" A familiar voice rang out.

"Papa!" Amy started forward.

"Amy! What are you doing here?!"

"I've been helping Grandpa," Amy said in a small voice.

"I thought you were in your bed!" Her father's voice had risen to a roar.

The crowd immediately became silent.

"Amy!" Grandpa turned toward her. "You didn't tell me!"

"I guess we're all suffering from ignorance tonight, Papa." Hans took a deep breath, calming himself. "Now, could someone please tell me what's going on?"

"We were just trying to get to the bottom of it ourselves," someone said.

"All I know is that I spent the day trying to fasten bits of sleigh to other, more rotten bits of sleigh, and I was finally testing the resulting piece of junk," Owen spoke up, "when we nearly collided with this sleigh." He chuckled. "The driver was kind enough to . . .

ummm . . . offer me a 'lift' when it became obvious that my mode of transport was not going to get me home."

Grandpa laughed and took up the story. "Amy and I completed our sleigh this afternoon and were taking it out for a test drive before presenting it to Santa. We'd have succeeded in keeping it a secret if we hadn't met Owen here."

"So this is the project you've been working on for the past four months?" Hans asked.

"It is, Papa!" Amy spoke up. "Isn't it beautiful?"

Hans moved closer, straining to see in the dim light. "It's a bit dark to tell right now," he said finally. "From what little I can see, it certainly looks like a beauty!"

More murmurs from the crowd.

"Are you saying that you believe this story, Hans?" someone said.

"Well *I* certainly do," Beany's voice broke in, suddenly. "I watched them carve it!" the small elf laughed sheepishly, "though I didn't know what it was. They told me it was some sort of large, adult-sized toy."

"And I believe it too," Hans added. "Papa taught Amy to carve, and I knew that they were working on something very secret. They would only tell me that it was going to benefit many, many people." He laughed. "I had no idea. I thought they had designed a new, revolutionary toy!"

"Well it *is* revolutionary," Grandpa said slowly, "but not in the way you think."

Hans laughed. "To think that *this* is what you have been working on!" He gripped Grandpa's arm and towed him along as he made a partial circuit of the sleigh. "I can't wait till it's light," he said. "It does look like a beauty!"

"I'm so excited for you to really see it, Papa!" Amy said. "It's the most beautiful sleigh anyone ever built!" She paused. "I carved the runners!"

"Oh, baby, did you really?"

"She did," Grandpa broke in. "And did a wonderful job too."

Hans knelt in the snow and ran his hand over the nearest runner. "It looks beautiful, honey," he said. "Now I really can't wait for the morning!"

He got to his feet. "Well, I think we've all had enough excitement," he said. "Let's take care of the reindeer and find our beds. Tomorrow promises to be . . . rather remarkable."

Ten

Grandpa pulled his heavy coat on over his sweater and retrieved his boots from beside the fireplace.

He paused at the bottom of his porch and tilted his face toward the sky. Light, wet flakes immediately soaked his skin. "Huh," he said. "Snowing. Heavily." He laughed. "My favorite type of weather."

"Good thing you live at the North Pole then, Papa," Hans's voice startled him.

He turned toward the sound, holding out his hand. "Hans! So glad you could join me!"

"And me too!" Amy's voice piped up. A small body threw itself against Grandpa's legs and squeezed hard.

"I wouldn't miss this for all the presents in Santa's sack," she whispered.

"I'm so glad you're here, partner," Grandpa said, leaning down and returning her hug. "We couldn't have started without you!"

"And I came along to make sure that the three of you stay out of trouble!" Carra said. She moved closer and gave Grandpa a hug as well. "So proud and happy today," she said softly.

"Thank you, my dear," Grandpa replied.

The four of them made their way through deepening snow to Grandpa's shop.

Hans swung the cargo doors open.

"How does she look in the light of day?" Grandpa asked.

Hans stepped into the room and stopped. "Beautiful!" he breathed.

"Oh, Papa Adam, more than beautiful!" Carra said. She moved past her husband. "Oh, it's the most beautiful thing I've ever seen!" She laughed softly. "And red seats! I think I can see my daughter's hand in that!"

"Are they red?" Grandpa turned to Amy.

"I like red," she said.

"Well, shall we pull it out?" Hans asked.

"Let's!" Carra said.

The four of them each grabbed the dangling traces and pulled. The sled slid smoothly across the floor and into the snow.

"Well, that was certainly easier than I expected!" Carra said, rather breathlessly. "Oh, Papa Adam, it's even more beautiful out here in the daylight!"

Grandpa smiled. "I'm so glad," he said simply.

"We did good, didn't we?" Amy asked.

"Oh, darling, you did remarkably well," her mother said. "In fact, I'd say the whole thing is a miracle!"

"And I would agree with you," Grandpa said softly.

He lifted his head. From somewhere came the jingling of harness bells. Several sets of harness bells.

"Wonder who that could be?" Hans laughed. "Why, hello, Dasher. So glad you could make it! Prancer, looking fit. Vixen, beautiful as always. Cupid, I knew you wouldn't be able to miss this! Blitzen and Dancer, already groomed, as usual. Comet, I almost didn't recognize you in your new collar! And Donner, late, as always. Good breakfast?"

A snort was his only answer.

"Everyone here? Should we carry on?" Grandpa asked.

Hans and Amy made short work of hitching up the reindeer.

"There we go," Hans said, dusting off his hands.

"All ready for Santa!" Amy sang out.

"Shall we get in?"

"That is a great idea!" Grandpa laughed. He waved his hand. "After you, my dears," he said.

The four of them scrambled inside, two to a seat, and sat back for the short ride to the main compound.

Dasher shook his bells and the reindeer leapt, as one, into the sky.

"Whoops!" Grandpa said, laughing, "that first hurdle always gets me. Or at least my stomach!"

The ride was very smooth but far too short. With hardly a bump, they were once more on the ground. And instantly surrounded by what sounded like every elf at the Pole.

"Wow. What a crowd!" Amy said softly into Grandpa's ear.

"Well, it's an important moment." He laughed. "And you don't get one of those every day!" He swung lightly out of the sleigh and waited for his family to join him.

"I wish my brothers and my other kids could be here to see this!" Hans said as he joined his father.

"Well, New York to the North Pole is a bit of a trip at the height of the season, son," Grandpa said. "But I agree. I wish they could be here too." He sighed. "And your mama."

"She would have loved this," Carra said, putting her arm gently through Grandpa's. "But I'm sure she's watching from somewhere!"

He smiled. "I know she is," he said softly.

The crowd suddenly went silent.

Grandpa lifted his head. Somewhere a door opened. And heavy footsteps squeaked through new snow.

"Well, what have we here?" a loud, jolly voice called out.

"It's a new sleigh, Santa!" Amy's voice rang out. "Your new sleigh that Grandpa and I made for you!"

"Well, I guess that about covers it!" Grandpa laughed. "Ummm . . . surprise!" he said weakly.

Santa laughed. That loud, rolling, jolly, perfect, "ho, ho, ho!" The heavy steps made their way around the sleigh and back. Then a large hand suddenly clapped down on Grandpa's shoulder. "And it's the most wonderful surprise I've ever had!" Santa said softly.

Grandpa smiled happily. Then he sobered. "Well, it comes with a bit of a story, Santa," he said.

"I love a story! Here, stand up on my porch! We'll all listen!"

Grandpa was conducted up several steps to a wooden platform. He heard Amy's light steps follow. He cleared his throat.

The crowd, which had been starting to stir, quieted once more.

"I guess I don't have to tell you how my blindness affected me," he began.

Complete silence.

"Everyone's watching you, Grandpa," Amy whispered loudly.

A couple of snickers from the crowd.

Grandpa half-smiled. "Well, suffice it to say that I was pretty much devastated and figured my useful life was as good as over." He reached out and touched the soft hair on his granddaughter's head. "And then, one day, Amy gave me a challenge I simply couldn't refuse."

"I told him that I wanted him to carve me something," Amy piped up. "Like he did for all of his other grandkids."

"She brought me a piece of wood that she had picked out herself."

"It was really pretty!" Amy added.

More snickers.

"After she left, I did something I never thought I'd do again. I dragged my toolbox out of the cupboard and got to work."

"He carved me an angel!" Amy crowed.

"An angel like my girl here."

"And just as I knew it would look," Amy added.

"And that's when I discovered that Amy had the gift," Grandpa went on. "She told me that the angel was just as she had seen it in the wood."

"Well, I *did* see it!" Amy broke in. "If you look at a pretty piece of wood, you can see whatever is in there, waiting for you to set it free."

"And that's what I've had to contend with." Grandpa laughed.

The crowd joined him.

"But I knew that she would be a carver," he went on when they had quieted down. "Like me, only better."

Amy scoffed softly. "No one's better than you, Grandpa!"

"So the two of us—handicapped, some of you would call us—began carving," he said, "and having some very pleasant days doing it."

"I carved lots of things. I even carved a bird for my mama!" Amy said, then clapped a hand over her mouth. "Oops."

The crowd laughed again.

"I guess I will forget I heard that!" Carra's voice came out of the crowd.

More laughter.

"Then Amy started telling me about the problems with Santa's sleigh," Grandpa went on, "and I came up with the idea of a new project. A big project. A new sleigh for Santa."

He smiled through tears. "And we did it." He paused. Then he swiped a hand over his face and sniffed. "I guess what I've really learned is this— don't ever think you are finished with life. Don't ever think that you can't do anything. Don't give up." He smiled. "Father Creator knows you and what you are capable of. He knows how you can contribute. He will find the way. What may look like a coincidence to you will be part of a plan, designed especially to help you."

He smiled and slid his hand onto Amy's shoulder, pressing her against his side. Then he lifted his head, gazing sightlessly out over the silent crowd, tears making tracks down his seamed cheeks. "He has angels. All sorts of angels. And he will send one of them to you, when you most need it."

He cleared his throat. "I've never seen my angel, but I know she is there." He patted Amy's head. "Helping me. Guiding me. Pushing me to be all I can be. All Father Creator expected me to be . . ." his voice died to a whisper, ". . . when he sent her."

He stepped back and bowed slightly.

The crowd cheered wildly, clapping, laughing, and calling out to the two on the steps.

Santa climbed the stairs and threw an arm around Grandpa's shoulders. He leaned forward. "Thank you, Papa Adam," he said softly into the aged ear. Then he reached out and gathered Amy in with his other arm. "And thank you too, Amy," he said.

"You're welcome!" Amy sang out.

Grandpa smiled.

Santa cleared his throat. "Well, I think we've put Papa Adam in the spotlight for long enough," he said. "It's time for a test drive!"

He squeezed Grandpa and Amy again. "Are you up for accompanying Santa on his first flight in the new sleigh?"

Other footsteps crossed the porch just then. Lighter. Smaller.

"With Mrs. Santa, of course." Santa laughed.

"I should hope so," Mrs. Santa said. "I've got my warm coat on and everything!"

They all laughed.

"Okay, everyone, make way!" Santa said loudly. "It's time to see how this new sleigh works!"

Grandpa and Amy were towed along in Santa's wake.

"Here we are, my dears," Santa said. "Climb up!"

Grandpa reached out, feeling the familiar sides of his sleigh.

"We women will sit in the back," Mrs. Santa said, pulling Amy to her. "You men take the front—and the wind!"

Soon they were all seated.

"Okay, Dasher! It's your show now!" Santa called out.

The sound of bells. Then immediately they were in the air.

Grandpa could feel the cool, wet drops of snow hit his face. He lifted it to the breeze.

"Ahhh. There's nothing like a good sleigh ride!" Santa sighed happily.

"And you haven't had anything like a good sleigh ride for years," Mrs. Santa spoke up. "Because you haven't had a good sleigh!"

Santa laughed. "Well, those days are certainly behind us! Take us over the herds, Dasher!" he called out.

The sleigh made a smooth near turn.

"You can't see this, Papa Adam," Santa said, "but the herds are right below us." He laughed. "They are all running to see."

"Well, many of them will one day be pulling this sleigh," Mrs. Santa said. "It's probably a good thing to watch how it behaves!"

"True," Santa laughed. He sat back. "Well, this is nice," he said.

"Nice? It's wonderful!" Mrs. Santa chimed in.

Amy giggled happily. "You really like it?"

"I think it's the finest sleigh I've ever seen!" Mrs. Santa said firmly. "And Santa does too."

Santa laughed. "You're right as usual, my dear," he said.

He leaned over to Grandpa and patted the frail shoulder. "It is the best gift I've ever received." He snorted softly. "And we let it happen!' he said, almost to himself.

"Beg pardon?" Grandpa asked.

Santa sighed. "You did this," he said. "You, Papa Adam."

"And me!"

"And our little Amy!" Santa laughed. "All this time, you could have been carving! But you gave up." He shook his head. "And we let you!"

Grandpa shrugged.

"You two have given us more than a sleigh today, my friend," Santa went on. "You have given us the greater gift of understanding."

Amy giggled, then leaned forward and put her arms around her Grandpa's neck. "Remember what you told me about Father Creator giving us . . . challenges to make us perfect?" she said softly into his ear.

Grandpa smiled. "I certainly do."

"Well, it's true!"

"How do you know, angel?"

"Because it happened to you!"

"To me?" Grandpa seemed to be having difficulty with his voice.

"Yes. Now you're perfect!"

Grandpa brushed at his blind eyes. "Oh, angel . . ."

"Perfect," she said.

Santa patted Grandpa's shoulder again and smiled. Then he leaned forward. "Dasher! Take us home!"

discussion questions

1. Why did Papa Adam give up carving? Blindness contributed, but was that the only reason?
2. Why did Papa Adam take up his knives again for Amy when he wouldn't for anyone else?
3. How did the community, at large, regard Papa Adam? Little Amy? How is this disclosed?
4. What is the status of the reindeer in the community? Explain.
5. How does the community handle problems? What does this say about them?
6. How does Papa Adam feel about family?
7. How would you describe the inhabitants of the North Pole? Santa? Mrs. Santa? Beany?

acknowledgments

All my life, I have loved the stories of Santa, second only to the stories of the Savior for self-less giving.

I have been raised on them. They have become a huge part of me.

I would like to take this opportunity to thank all who have kept, and still keep, the idea of Santa alive. Who have consciously or unconsciously realized that, in the stories of Santa, we can find stories illustrating true service.

True love.

I want to be like that.

about the author

Diane Stringam Tolley was born and raised on a ranch in Southern Alberta, Canada. Educated in journalism, she is the author of countless articles and short stories and a novel for young adults, *Essence*. She and her husband, Grant, are the parents of six children and live in Beaumont, Alberta, Canada.